Copyright © 2004 by Claudia Graziano   26410-GRAZ
Book design by Michelle Barbera
ISBN: Softcover   1-4134-6652-4
              Hardcover   1-4134-6653-2

This is a work of fiction. Names, characters, places and incidents
either are the product of the author's imagination or are used
fictitiously, and any resemblance to any actual persons, living or
dead, events, or locales is entirely coincidental. This book was
printed in the United States of America.

To order additional copies of this book, contact:
Xlibris Corporation
1-888-795-4274
www.Xlibris.com
Orders@Xlibris.com

Meerkat's
SAFARI

By Claudia Graziano

Illustrated by Michelle Barbera

Inspired by Dan Sweeney

For the animals of the world

Pack your bags
and grab your hat.

Let's go on safari!
Follow me, the meerkat.

I'll take you to places
where animals run free.

Listen for clues
and guess who we might see.

This gentle beast peeks over treetops with ease.

Can you guess who likes to nibble on leaves?

8

Giraffes

When giraffes are thirsty,
they bend down low.

Eighteen feet tall
giraffes sometimes grow.

They close their noses
to keep out dust and sand.

Giraffes live in herds,
and sleep while they stand.

Out on the plains this king is hard to miss.

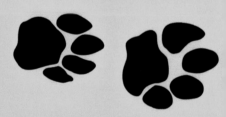

What kind of cat would rather roar than hiss?

Lions

Lions are fierce
and big and strong.

They hunt at night
and then sleep all day long.

Lions see in the dark
with eyes that glow.

Two lions rub cheeks
to say, "Hello!"

This creature glides and slides on its tail.

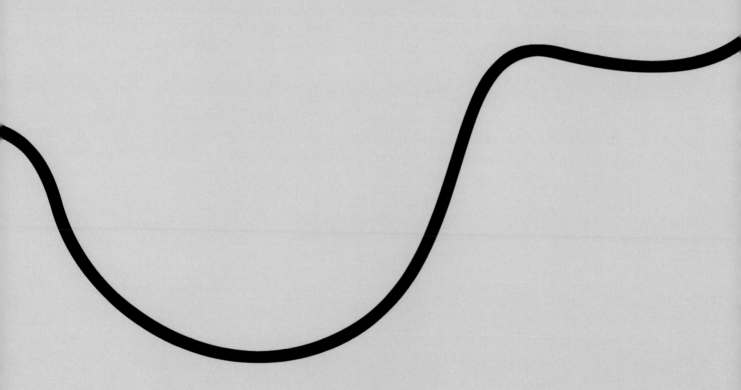

Do you know who, instead of fur, has scales?

Snakes

Snakes can crawl,
coil, climb and swim.

Several times a year
snakes shed their skin.

Some snakes are short,
some are as long as a bus.

Some snakes have fangs
but not all are poisonous.

This fellow has ears that flap in the breeze.

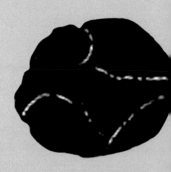

Who do you think sounds a trumpet with a sneeze?

Elephants

Elephants are
the largest mammals on land.

Their noses, called trunks,
they use like a hand.

Elephants can live
to be 60 years old.

Elephants get stomach aches
when the weather is cold.

21

Not a parrot, a peacock or a chickadee. . .

What feathered friend has webbed feet and pink knees?

23

Flamingos

Flamingos are known
for their long skinny legs.

In nests of mud
they lay a single white egg.

Flamingos prefer
salty marshes and seas.

They mingle in groups
called colonies.

25

Try to guess this one, its name is the key:

Who do you suppose is more like you than me?

Monkeys

Monkeys are noisy
and smart and fun.

They like to eat fruit
and laze in the sun.

Monkeys can swing
from tree to tree.

They use their long tails
for balance, you see.

This neighbor calls out with a snort and a bray.

Can you tell me who tends to blend with the shade?

Zebras

Zebras have stripes
so they can easily hide.

Lions and leopards
they watch for, wide-eyed.

Zebras, like horses,
love to eat grass.

They're feisty and wild
and run very fast.

Congratulations!

Our safari is done.
You've guessed all my friends
and met every one.

Until our next adventure
it's time for me to go.

Take a trip to the zoo,
there are more animals to know.

Claudia Graziano is a San Francisco-based freelance writer, editor and animal lover. A former middle school teacher, Ms. Graziano hopes her book will reinforce early language skills and promote repeat reading, as well as arouse kids' curiosity about animals and their sometimes eccentric behaviors.

Michelle Barbera is a Boston-based illustrator, graphic designer and meerkat enthusiast. This is her first children's book. Visit Ms. Barbera's online portfolio at *http://www.barberaillustration.com.*